# Successful Selling
# on the Internet

*in a week*

*Carol A. O'Connor*

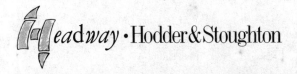
*Headway* · Hodder & Stoughton

# Acknowledgements

The author wishes to acknowledge and thank Network Wizards for permission to report their survey data and Georgia Tech Research Corporation for the licence to refer to data from the GVU Center's Fifth WWW User Survey.

Special thanks to:

- Scott Rawls for his enthusiasm and influence;
- Marilyn O'Connor for her excellent and tireless research;
- Brian Williams at CIX Compulink for his helpful remarks; and
- Jean O'Connor for her continued support.

*A catalogue record for this title is available from the British Library*

ISBN 0 340 67397 4

First published 1996
Impression number    10  9  8  7  6  5  4  3  2  1
Year                      1999    1998  1997  1996

Typeset by Multiplex Techniques Ltd, St Mary Cray, Kent. Printed in Great Britain for Hodder & Stoughton Educational, a division of Hodder Headline Plc, 338 Euston Road, London NW1 3BH by Redwood Books, Trowbridge, Wiltshire.

**the Institute**
**of Management**

*F O U N D A T I O N*

The Institute of Management (IM) is at the forefront of management development and best management practice. The Institute embraces all levels of management from students to chief executives. It provides a unique portfolio of services for all managers, enabling them to develop skills and achieve management excellence.

For information on the benefits of membership, please contact:

Department HS
Institute of Management
Cottingham Road
Corby
Northants NN17 1TT
Tel: 01536 204222
Fax: 01536 201651

This series is commissioned by the Institute of Management Foundation.

# C O N T E N T S

**Introduction**                                                    5

**Sunday**          Understanding the marketspace           7

**Monday**          Getting connected                       21

**Tuesday**         Identifying Internet benefits            38

**Wednesday**       The World Wide Web                       51

**Thursday**        Developing a home page                   62

**Friday**          Getting customers' attention             73

**Saturday**        Planning for action                      85

**Internet addresses**                                       89

**Author's recommendations**                                 90

**Further reading**                                          91

**Glossary**                                                 92

The Internet is such big news that it is difficult to remember a time when it was not on the media's agenda. However, it is far from being a fad. A closer look reveals a steady and gradual growth from its beginnings in the 1960s up to the mid-1980s with widespread public interest mushrooming only in the early 1990s. The Internet's rise to fame is less like a seven-day wonder and more like the sudden discovery of a film star who has actually been performing on stage for more than 20 years. This is reassuring because as businesses begin using the Internet now, they find an electronic infrastructure that is superbly maintained as well as responsibly planned by astonishingly clever people.

The Internet offers a direct and informal way for the average person to cut through bureaucracies and cross national borders almost without effort, as well as to gather information from the most prestigious sources in the world. It is as easy and no more expensive to send a message to a colleague across the street than it is to contact a supplier in Peru or a customer in Paris as long as they have an Internet connection.

*Selling* on the Internet is still a pioneering effort led largely by self-taught enthusiasts. Although they have no assurance of profit, the attitude they bring to discovering opportunities can only lead to a positive outcome. They are like New World explorers who are willing to take the risks and therefore will ultimately receive the rewards. This book is written to encourage others to join them. It offers a step-by-step guide to addressing the question: how can new technology be used to create sales, serve customers and develop business? It is a practical guide which presents the steps to successful selling on the Internet so that these can be explored during the course of a week. Each day brings a new topic, and by the end of the programme, all of the following essential issues will be covered:

| *Steps to successful selling on the Internet* | |
| --- | --- |
| **Sunday** | Understanding the marketspace |
| **Monday** | Getting connected |
| **Tuesday** | Identifying Internet benefits |
| **Wednesday** | The World Wide Web |
| **Thursday** | Developing a home page |
| **Friday** | Getting customers' attention |
| **Saturday** | Planning for action |

# Understanding the marketspace

The Internet is a collection of fully independent computer networks located around the world. Together they voluntarily form a single, giant system, with each individual network taking responsibility for its own administration and maintenance and each setting its own priorities. It is a source of wonder that the Internet is based upon the cooperation of these separate and distinct networks, and that its considerable success is the result of informal agreements. The result is an emerging international forum called the marketspace.

Today's chapter gives an overview of the Internet's development, and includes a sample diagram of a typical computer network making a connection to the Internet's mainline system (see page 14). It also presents survey results about who is using the Internet, with data highlighting how it has grown during the last five years. Finally, key questions are asked that will help company leaders decide if Internet selling is right for them.

- From education to commerce
- The Information Superhighway
- Who uses the Internet?
- Is Internet selling for you?

## From education to commerce

Thirty years ago, the major investor in network technology was the US military searching for ways to protect its defence data from nuclear attack. Its strategy was to locate several *supercomputers* around the country, and to link these via high-capacity electronic cable so that they could share memory power, minimise repetition of tasks and reduce the government's risk of losing a single, centrally located computer. There were also cost-cutting benefits associated with shared computer use which made this solution very attractive, and gradually major US research universities and government agencies such as NASA began using the emerging network technology as well. Highly creative individuals were called upon to invent ways to connect very different computer systems, and this enabled the development of *free standing networks*, each sharing information while also maintaining a separate identity. The spirit of enthusiasm, adventure and creative expression characterising this early period contributed directly to the Internet's rapid rate of growth.

It is the Internet's lack of central authority or corporate policy which puzzles some business leaders, and there are stories of managers asking to speak to the Internet's managing director. For some, the Internet's lack of regulation is not only frustrating but also very difficult to understand or accept. However, this hasn't stopped many adventurous managers from exploring how the Internet can increase sales and improve their commercial activity in general. These are the pioneers who not only sense a new way to do business but also want to satisfy their personal curiosity. Their enthusiasm for the medium – even when describing their electronic crises, mistakes and crashes – is often contagious and has certainly contributed to the rapid increase in the number of commercial users of the Internet.

*Shifts in registered usage*

The following data is selected from surveys conducted by Network Wizards (see the 'Internet addresses' section), and is chosen to show the way the Internet has grown during the last five years. Each number represents a *computer system* registered under a single name and address rather than the *number of people* who gain access to the Internet by using that address. It is impossible to say how many *actual* users there are for each of these systems because some addresses represent departments of very large companies or a single Internet connection shared by several users. It is safe, however, to assume that there is at least one user for each of the systems represented by the following figures.

|                 | 1991    | 1996      |
|-----------------|---------|-----------|
| Educational     | 243,020 | 1,793,491 |
| Commercial      | 181,361 | 2,430,954 |
| Government      | 46,463  | 312,330   |
| Military        | 27,492  | 258,791   |
| Organisations   | 19,117  | 265,327   |
| UK              | 18,984  | 451,750   |
| Network systems | 4,109   | 758,597   |

These figures show that between 1991 and 1996, registered Internet use shifted dramatically from educational to commercial activity: with commercial usage growing by more than 13 times and educational usage increasing by more than 7 times. Further, this data shows only a *part* of actual commercial growth because many European businesses register under their country's name rather than under the category 'com' which stands for 'commercial'. For example, UK registration is nearly 24 times larger today than five years ago, and although many of the new users are private individuals, much of this increase is very likely to be in business activity.

*Who is investing?*
This interest in commercial usage has caused serious concern among some of the Internet's educational users and developers who suggest that the companies now investing in network technology could easily decide to raise the fees they charge for Internet connections, with the

result that non-business users become gradually choked out of the game. In reply, however, it can be said that these new investors will only generate profits if their networks are used by a wide enough variety of customers from individual users to large businesses.

This response, indeed, is supported by the kind of investment being made. This includes developing the Internet's infrastructure by adding *backbone cables*, the super-powerful lines to which smaller networks connect. In 1991 in the US, the Commercial Internet Association (CIX) was formed by three leading electronic technology firms. These firms agreed, along with many other networks, to advance commercial usage on all Internet segments falling outside of US government funding. In Europe, there is an equal commitment to developing new commercial backbone lines. In 1995, EUnet offered a powerful new high-capacity line primarily for commercial users. This enhances an already well-developed system which includes several powerful lines, including the EuropaNET which is used exclusively to link European national universities.

Interested business people can join the debate about the Internet's future and its growth by contacting the Internet Society (see the 'Internet addresses' section) which promotes the evolution of the Internet through education and technology support, and provides a forum for developing new Internet applications. Membership is open and attracts people from a wide range of backgrounds, including programmers, educators, business people and general enthusiasts.

## The Information Superhighway

The idea that data *travels* along cable and wires and across airwaves has inspired many politicians and media people to describe the Internet as an *Information Superhighway*. This charismatic image has done much to interest non-computer users in the Internet, and is therefore very positive. The term's main limitation, on the other hand, is the confusion it causes by implying that there are actual physical locations on the Internet which people can visit to make a purchase or to contact other users. This is no more possible than a visit to the *Starship Enterprise*, and even sophisticated users tend to forget this. Although it is more accurate to describe the Internet as a highly complex pattern of fibre optic lines, high-speed telephone cables, radio waves and satellite contacts, all linked together electronically, this provides a less than vivid and colourful image – and is far too long a description to provide a good sound byte.

An alternative approach describes the *relationship* between planet earth and the Internet. This is rather like a tennis ball slowly being wrapped with string until finally the surface of the ball disappears. The string and the ball *together* form the Internet because the wiring by itself has no value and no purpose unless there are *people* using the electronic networks which now cover the earth's surface. The diagram on the following page shows the kinds of equipment and wiring connections which are typically found in a network. Definitions for each of these components are given below.

*Backbones:* ultra-high-capacity fibre optic lines which transmit data to and from major computer sites around the world.

*T-1 and T-3:* special high-speed and heavy-traffic lines which connect networks to the Internet backbones through router (see below) computers.

*Telephone lines:* standard and special (ISDN) lines which link computers to router computers.

*Routers:* computers which connect networks of different types and serve to transmit messages beyond a sender's local area.

*Mainframes:* very large computers with fast processing speed and high-capacity data storage. In large companies, data processing is centralised by connecting individual computer terminals to the mainframe.

*Bridges:* computers which provide a connection for other computers within a local area so that they can work together and share information.

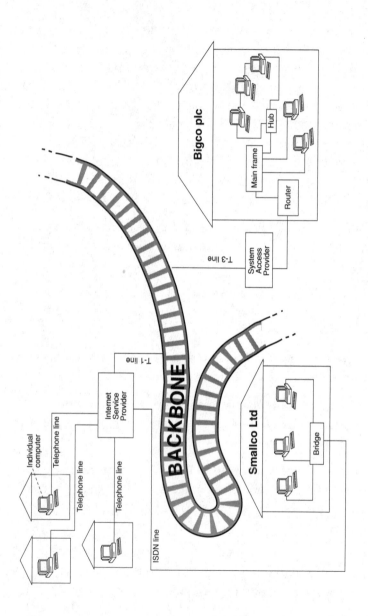

*Hubs:* computers which tie other computers together to allow them to combine their memory and work together to process information beyond their individual capacity.

*Individual computers:* these can either connect directly to the Internet or form links, through hubs or bridges, which connect them indirectly to the Internet.

## Who uses the Internet?

All of the above-mentioned cables, lines and supercomputers provide the means to connect ordinary people and organisations to the Internet. The data below shows Internet growth during the last 10 years, and once again is taken from Network Wizards' Internet surveys which have been conducted regularly since 1981. As mentioned before, each number represents a registered *computer system* and so could indicate thousands of *actual users*. Data from other Internet user surveys indicates that there could be as many as 30 million actual Internet users world-wide.

| | | | |
|---|---|---|---|
| August 1981 | 213 | October 1991 | 617,000 |
| October 1984 | 1,024 | October 1992 | 1,136,000 |
| November 1986 | 5,089 | October 1993 | 2,056,000 |
| December 1987 | 28,174 | October 1994 | 3,864,000 |
| October 1989 | 159,000 | January 1996 | 9,472,000 |

Those deciding whether or not to use the Internet for sales purposes need to know as much as possible about all these users. Are they just 'sad anoraks' with nothing better to do but sit in front of a computer screen? Do they have money to spend, and if so, what kind of sales can businesses expect to make? The following data on Internet users partially answers these questions. It is taken from the GVU (Graphics, Visualization and Usability) Center's (see the 'Internet addresses' section) Survey conducted in April and May 1996, and is based on more than 11,700 responses.

| Average age | | Marital status | |
|---|---|---|---|
| All users | 33.0 years | Married | 41.1% |
| Europeans | 28.8 years | Single | 40.8% |
| Weekend users | 33.4 years | | |

| Proportion of use by gender | | Average income | |
|---|---|---|---|
| Total of females | 31.5% | All users | £38,000 |
| Total of males | 68.5% | European users | £32,000 |
| Females 16–20 years | 12.9% | | |
| Males 16–20 years | 10.1% | | |

| Occupations | | | |
|---|---|---|---|
| Computer industry | 27.8% | Management | 10.7% |
| Education | 29.6% | Other | 13.0% |
| Professions | 18.9% | | |

Among this survey's many findings is the suggestion that *Internet browsing* is replacing television with 36% reporting a preference for 'surfing' the Internet over watching television. Many users of all age groups consider this browsing to be a leisure activity. It is also interesting that 80% of those surveyed visited the Internet each day, but that only 14.2% of them used the Internet for shopping. This last finding could be the result of security fears which 60% of the surveyed users said was the primary cause of their not buying merchandise through the Internet.

The following data highlights the uses these visitors find for their Internet connections. Those surveyed could choose more than one activity.

| Uses for Internet connections | |
|---|---|
| General browsing | 78.7% |
| Entertainment | 64.5% |
| Work | 50.9% |
| Shopping | 14.2% |

## Is Internet selling for you?

During the Internet's formative years, developing an Internet sales programme has not necessarily been the right decision for everyone. The following questionnaire addresses key issues for consideration before making investment in time or new equipment. Each of these issues is explored during the week's programme of activities.

1 Are you willing to experiment and take controlled risks in order to gain new business?

     Yes?          No?          Maybe?

2 Do you recognise the risks of making sales through anonymous Internet contacts?

     Yes?          No?          Maybe?

3 Are you willing to respond to comments received directly and immediately from customers?

     Yes?          No?          Maybe?

4 Do you want to use the Internet to strengthen relationships with present and potential customers?

     Yes?          No?          Maybe?

5 Do your products appeal directly to the age groups of current Internet users?

     Yes?          No?          Maybe?

6 Do you have allies among your suppliers or producers of complementary goods and services with whom you could share Internet contacts?

     Yes?          No?          Maybe?

7 Are you willing to give free information and advice on topics related to your product?

     Yes?          No?          Maybe?

8 Is your company in a position to act on new ideas and is it prepared to change?

     Yes?          No?          Maybe?

9 Are you and your colleagues enthusiastic enough to manage the frustration which goes along with technology setbacks during the Internet's pioneering stages?

     Yes?             No?             Maybe?

10 Can your product or service be sold nationally and internationally, or can you think of new products for a wider market?

     Yes?             No?             Maybe?

## Scores

Add up the total number of 'Yes', 'No' and 'Maybe' answers:

- *'Yes' scores of 8 to 10* show a strong likelihood that Internet selling is right for your company

- *'Yes' scores of 4 to 7* indicate the need for further information and analysis before any investments are made

- *'Yes' scores of 1 to 3* indicate that Internet selling could be very challenging for you and your company. A review of how this new medium of Internet selling fits into an overall sales strategy would be beneficial before any steps are taken

- *'Maybe' scores of 5 to 10* indicate a need to consider what you hope to gain from an Internet sales programme. No action should be taken until all of the 'Maybe' scores become either 'Yes' or 'No'

## Summary

Today's chapter has looked at how the Internet's primary usage has changed from education and research to commerce. It has also introduced issues relating to techonology which will be explored more fully tomorrow.

# Getting connected

In theory, anyone with a computer, a telephone and a piece
of connecting equipment can create a link to the Internet. In
practice, it's a little more difficult. At its worst it's rather
like piecing together a do-it-yourself furniture kit with
missing instructions and a lack of tools.

Today's chapter is about making a successful Internet
connection with a minimum of unnecessary expense and
frustration. It offers an overview of the issues which need
decisions, including equipment purchasing or upgrading,
cable and wiring investments to initiate a link, and the kind
of services which will be required from either an Internet
Service Provider or a System Access Provider in order to
carry on business activity. It also explains what actually
happens electronically when connections to the Internet are
made, and where and how selling transactions take place in

a world of wiring, cables and computer memory chips. The topics in today's chapter thus include:

- The virtual world: fact and fiction
- Examining technology needs
- Decision-making essentials

## The virtual world: fact and fiction

The Internet is a *virtual world* where ideas begin to seem as tangible as physical things and where flickering images allow people to contact each other in new ways. It is easy to forget that this dream world assumes an 'existence' only when users turn on their computers and press buttons in search of information. This information *lives* or is stored on computer chips and is no more robust than a movie videotape still resting inside its plastic case. Both of these electronic media need electricity, machinery and a human user before a meaningful world of image and colour can be created.

The opportunity to contact other people informally and directly is a valuable Internet benefit which lends substance to the idea that the Internet is more than a bunch of information files. Imagination, sparkle, responsiveness and flexibility are what make the Internet an interesting and entertaining place to do business. These qualities are like modern-day muses acting as a positive influence on any selling effort.

## Examining technology needs

Anyone with an *automatic teller machine* (ATM) card has
already mastered the skill of connecting to a computer
network. By entering their cards and a password into an
ATM, banking customers send a signal to the bank's entire
computer network, as well as to the networks of other
banks if these are also needed for the transaction. This
process is possible because banks, world-wide, have been
connected to electronic networks for many years. Now, this
same technology is also available for home or office use.

*Taking the first steps*
Contact to the Internet can be arranged in a variety of
ways. The first steps should be taken carefully and be
based on long-term company needs so that any choices
about equipment and wiring connections are made in line
with the company's overall vision and its goals for growth,
sales, communication and customer service. Where any of

these issues are unclear, top company leaders should sit down and clarify where they want their business to go and how they imagine the Internet can help them to get there.

This approach saves wasted time, money and effort because so often the right technology solution emerges when *human ambitions* are identified first. A hard look at what the company wants to achieve through an Internet connection often leads to the priority setting necessary to find the money to pay for the investment. The costs involved can range from a low operational cost with minor equipment purchase at the entry level of commitment, to a mid-level of cost with some investment in equipment at the developmental stage of commitment, to the need to hire operational staff, install new wiring and invest extensively in new equipment at the full level of commitment.

Here is a summary of the requirements for each investment level, followed by explanations for each of the new terms used:

*Entry level*

- Wiring:
  - a standard dial-up telephone line
- Equipment:
  - a computer – anything from an elderly model to a whizz-bang modern model
  - a modem with the highest rate of speed available
- Service:
  - a telephone connection to a local Internet Service Provider

*Developmental level*

- Wiring:
  - a dedicated telephone line, ISDN line or leased line from a local Internet Service Provider
- Equipment:
  - a powerful computer with a high-speed processor and memory capacity
  - a modem, ISDN terminal adapter or router computer, depending on the kind of line
- Service:
  - a line connection to a local Internet Service Provider

*Fully committed level*

- Wiring:
  - a dedicated high-capacity line
- Equipment:
  - in-house company computer network with router computers connecting to an Internet backbone
- Service:
  - a line connection leased directly from a System Access Provider

*Wiring*
A standard dial-up telephone line

This is exactly what it says it is. A connection to the Internet can be made by linking the computer to a telephone through a modem (see the 'Equipment' section below). Whenever a user wants to connect to the Internet, they dial a telephone number given to them by their Internet Service Provider (see the 'Service' section below). Every minute used during an Internet connection is billed to the telephone line as if it were an ordinary phone call. An existing business phone or the office fax line can be used, but use of these lines for Internet access ties them up so that incoming calls or faxes get a busy signal.

A dedicated dial-up telephone line

This just means adding another dial-up line which is used only for Internet access.

An ISDN line

This means an Integrated Services Digital Network line, and it is the next available upgrade from a standard telephone line. Essentially, it doubles the speed of data transfer and offers a more reliable connection so that the call is less likely to be cut off halfway through transmission. A regular telephone line needs a modem in order to translate *digital* data (zeros and ones) from the computer into *analogue* data in the form of sounds which travel along local phone lines as chirps, beeps and tones. At the main telephone switchboards, these sounds must then be converted back into digital data for long-distance transmission. An ISDN connection is able to take the digital data directly from the computer and transmit it as digital *signals* to telephone switchboards world-wide. By thus avoiding the switch from digital to analogue, computer data is less likely to become corrupted or lost.

A leased line

This kind of line is usually categorised according to its speed, and this starts at about the speed of an ISDN line. The fastest lines are fibre optic and are very fast indeed. This kind of connection is primarily for businesses requiring a 24-hour Internet connection with high speed and maximum data-transfer reliability. It is a necessity if a business plans to connect its own internal network of computers to the Internet.

The leased line is the most expensive option and requires: new computer equipment to connect the company's internal system to the line; premium line rental costs; ongoing connection costs to either an Internet Service Provider or a System Access Provider (see the 'Service' section below); and rental of connection equipment from this provider. On the positive side, individual calls are not charged, and so a business intending to use its Internet connection for more than three hours per day can benefit. A leased line also allows a company to take better advantage of the Internet as a means of improving communication among its staff who are spread apart geographically.

*Equipment*
Computers

In practice, users can connect even elderly computer models to the Internet and, through their Service Provider, present perfectly adequate sales promotions. Unfortunately, these older machines generally predate the ability to use pictures, graphics and sound, and so unless this equipment can be upgraded, sales presentations prepared on these machines are likely to depend upon text on a black and white screen. Even so, where necessary, users *can* begin their Internet selling experience with the machines they already have.

Although the 'Author's recommendations' section on page 91 makes general equipment suggestions, Internet technology is improving so quickly that more specific proposals are unlikely to be helpful. However, faster and more powerful equipment is generally better because this cuts operating costs and enables presentation of attractive promotions. Sunday's chapter referred to hubs, bridges and routers as computers with special network functions, and described what they are and how they contribute to network technology. Because of their expense, these computers should be purchased as part of an overall plan which also takes into account the need to invest in wiring, the cost of the Internet service connection and company goals for growth and development.

## Modems

The word modem stands for *modulator – demodulator* and refers to its function of translating digital (computer) data into analogue signals (sounds) so that the data can then travel along standard telephone lines. For business use, the fastest available modem is best. This currently means choosing a minimum speed of 28.8 bps (bits per second).

There are two kinds of modem: internal and external.

1 *Internal:* many new computer models have internal modems already installed. These are small rectangular pieces of metal which are embedded with computer chips and fitted inside the computer. Alternatively, internal modems can be purchased so that they can be installed in do-it-yourself fashion in the office, although this is always more difficult than the manufacturers suggest. Internal modems for full-size computers are not designed to be transferred from one computer to another after they are installed, but those designed for portable computers, called *modem cards*, are easily removed and can be used in another portable.

2   *External:* these are usually connected to the computer
    with a plug and cable. External modems can be easily
    moved from one computer to another and are generally
    robust in design. Many provide sets of signal lights to
    show the status of outgoing and incoming messages.
    These signals are extremely useful for beginners because
    they clearly indicate the status of the data being
    transmitted.

Helplines

Before buying a modem, make sure that its manufacturer
provides a nationally based customer-support telephone
number with at least 9-to-5 access. Many do not. Technical
support is essential even for experienced computer users
because installation is not always as straightforward as it
should be, and it can be a hair-pulling, teeth-gnashing
experience to discover that the modem doesn't quite match
the computer's expectations. After the modem is physically
plugged into the computer, it also has a software program
which must be installed so that the computer can identify
the kind of modem it is and then work cooperatively with
its unique features. However, each modem brand comes
with its own software, and this is where difficulties arise.
*Easy learning* tutorials explaining how to plug in a cable are
of little help if the more important issue of computer–
modem compatibility is not resolved. A helpline
representative should be able to give coding information
and installation advice so that a brief telephone call can sort
out this kind of difficulty in minutes.

ISDN terminal adapter

This provides a link between the computer and an ISDN
line. It is different from a modem in that it accepts
incoming and outgoing digital data *without* the need to
translate this into analogue signals for the telephone line.
These adapters, at the time of writing, are at least three
times as expensive as modems.

*Service*
Internet Service Providers

Until the mid-1980s, connections to the Internet were made
through universities, government offices and the military.
Only these organisations had the resources to purchase the
very expensive earlier generations of computers. However,
with the development of programs and equipment which
enable data transfer along the national telephone system,
and with the growing ownership of personal computers
and Apple Macs, the communication benefits that the
Internet offers became more readily accessible to
individuals and smaller groups. In time, this led to the
creation of a new service industry, the Internet Service
Provider (ISP).

Because national telephone systems weren't designed to
provide direct connections between personal computers
and Internet mainline cables, ISPs are needed to act as
*gateways*. They use purpose-designed computers which
accept data along telephone lines from less powerful home
and office computers and then route this onto the faster
long-distance cable. ISPs charge a fee both for providing an
Internet access point and for a variety of special services
such as business research, newspaper and journal

highlights, and financial market information. Some services such as electronic mail (e-mail) are standard across all servers.

When choosing a server, the whole package of services needs assessment before any commitment can be made. Although it is technically easy to change servers, this can cause inconvenience and increase the chance of errors occurring for customers. The larger ISPs lease ISDN and high-speed fibre optic lines to businesses. If a company plans to expand its internet commitment, then its choice of server should also be based on the ISP's line-leasing capacity both present and future.

Another vital issue is the *bandwidth* of the server's connection to the backbone system. This refers to a line's capacity to carry data at speed, and it can be discovered by learning who is its System Access Provider (see below) and asking what is its bandwidth capability. An adequate bandwidth enables users to access the company's promotions with a minimum wait. An inadequate bandwidth can mean long waits for users or, worse, their receipt of a 'failure to connect' message. This is not only frustrating for them but is also an embarrassment for the company.

System Access Providers

Large companies with national or international offices, many employees and internal networks require leased lines and should explore connecting directly to the Internet backbone system. For this, they should contact one of the commercial access providers. The investment in equipment and wiring installation required here becomes cost-effective where maximum reliability, speed and intensive usage are important issues. Among the System Access Providers are EUnet, BTnet and Unipalm PIPEX (see the 'Internet addresses' section).

Gaining correct information often depends upon asking the right questions. The following list of questions focuses on the issues businesses should address when choosing a service provider. The first set of questions apply to Internet Service Providers and the second set to System Access Providers.

1   Contact at least five Internet Service Providers (lists of these can be found in any Internet magazine) and ask them the following questions:

 • Do they have a local contact number?
 • Are there no more than 30 users for each incoming line at the server's end?

- Are they a member of any organisation made up of service providers which ensures good Internet connections?
- Do they lease their lines directly from a commercial backbone system?
- At what speeds are they able to transmit data through their links to the backbone system?
- Do they specialise in services for business?
- Do they charge:
  - flat rates
  - per service used
  - measured use
  - flat rate plus measured use?
- Do they make memory available for the development of promotional sites?
- Do they allow customers to use their Internet connection for commercial purposes?
- Do they provide helpline support? If so, at which hours?

2  Contact System Access Providers and ask them the following questions:

- What plans do they have to enhance their infrastructure in order to improve technology for customers?
- Who are their main investors and developers?
- What leased lines are available in terms of speed and capacity? At what cost?
- What technical support is available? At what cost?
- What percentage of their customers are in business? Do they deal with government bodies? Do they deal with educational institutions?

- Does any one customer base receive preference over the others?
- What router equipment do you have to acquire for your use in-house?
- What router equipment are you required to lease or buy from the provider for use at their location?
- Does their governing charter impose any limitations on usage?
- Do they foresee any changes in their ownership, governmental policy or technical upgrade requirements for your company in the near future?

## Decision-making essentials

The following questions highlight decision-making areas essential when planning an Internet connection. A general suggestion for initial action follows each question. Because individual companies have specialised needs, these suggestions should only serve as examples of the kinds of decision which should be made.

1  *Are you an individual selling services which you perform yourself?*

Begin with a high-speed modem connection through a telephone line to a commercial Internet Service Provider. Upgrade your computer's memory and processing ability to make data transfer speedier.

2  *Are you an individual with a catalogue of products to sell?*

Refer to the above suggestion and add colour and graphics capability so that you can produce and

transmit attractively presented electronic brochures for
transmission to your service provider for storage and
24-hour access to potential customers.

3   *Are you a small-to-medium-sized business, with a well-
developed computer system already organised into an in-house
network, now wishing to use the Internet to promote products
and services?*

Use your bridge computer to make a single ISDN-line or
leased-line connection to your service provider for
reliable and dedicated links. You will need a terminal
adapter rather than a modem for an ISDN line. If your
in-house computer system is not yet on a network but
this *is* part of your long-term plans, look for a bridge
computer with the capacity to work with a leased-line
connection rather than getting a bridge, a terminal
adapter and an ISDN line – this may be a more cost-
effective and efficient solution.

4   *Are you a medium-sized company retailing an extensive
product line, planning to conduct market research, inviting
customer feedback and needing an internal communication
system?*

Consider linking several computers into a hub and
connecting this through a powerful bridge computer to
other hubs, each with a specialist function. The bridge
would provide the main link to the Internet Service
Provider from which you would lease a private line.

5 *Are you a large company with a well-known brand name already using the Internet for communication and research, and now wishing to begin using it for product promotion?*

Examine your system's current capability and discuss upgrade requirements for marketing with the IT manager. Contact System Access Providers to discuss a direct link through one of them to the backbone system. You will also need a powerful router computer to connect the company's system to the backbone, and to pay for wiring installation as well. Other in-house equipment upgrades may also be necessary.

## Summary

Today's chapter has provided an overview of the equipment, wiring and service issues which a business needs to address in order to sell on the Internet. Tomorrow's chapter will explore the benefits of an Internet connection.

# Identifying Internet benefits

The main criterion for successful selling on the Internet is a willingness to re-evaluate conventional ideas about how customers behave; what attracts them to a product or service; and what information they want about it before they choose to buy. Today's chapter addresses these issues by exploring how the Internet is different from other sales media, and looks closely at the ways many companies now present product-related information as a customer service. Examples of Internet selling schemes are presented in order to highlight what kind of selling effort works on the Internet and what does not. Finally, positive and negative features of Internet selling are assessed. The day's topics thus include:

- Empowering the user
- Using information to add value
- Analysing what works
- Internet pros and cons

## Empowering the user

The Internet is highly democratic in that its users can communicate at will to virtually any other user on equal terms. Current technology offers an enormous degree of power and, in general, Internet users know this. Being able to respond immediately to what is on the screen is part of the Internet's attraction. In this respect, the Internet differs from radio, television, newspapers and magazines because it invites *two-way* communication between buyers and sellers. The telly-watcher who shouts 'rubbish!' at a patently stupid commercial can take this remark no further, but the Internet user who wants to comment on a product or service and how it is promoted can always find a way to do so. Those companies wise enough to present sales promotions so that they invite feedback not only acknowledge customer power but also gain access to a veritable gold mine of information for product improvement and increased customer satisfaction (see Thursday's chapter, pages 62–72).

A single Internet connection offers a company the following range of services:

- *Sales:* providing product information; taking orders and payments 24 hours a day
- *Market research:* immediate information from the world press; a potential for low-cost customer-satisfaction surveys and the ability to gain voluntary feedback

- *E-mail:* high-speed electronic mail which provides efficient, speedy written communication between sales people, administrators and production people, the distribution department and all in-house staff, as well as a direct line of communication to even the most senior company leaders
- *Electronic brochures:* the ability to provide on-screen catalogues of entire product lines, with the further capability of daily updates
- *Promotion:* on-screen presentations to highlight products and attract business, with 24-hour-a-day access for potential customers
- *Information services:* providing information which highlights a product's usefulness and value in a colourful and interesting way, and also draws attention to related topics which both inform and interest potential customers

Although sales, market research and promotion are available through other media, they are transformed on the Internet because technology allows a business to focus intently on the buyers' convenience at little or no added cost. The other sales services on the above list are the direct result of the computer's ability to store vast amounts of information and then transmit it on request. The main ingredient for success is to organise this information so that potential buyers can gain easy access to the product details they want. Those companies which build into their promotions a sense that they have anticipated their customers' needs in order to better serve them enhance their image and create brand loyalty for their products. No other sales media empowers the customer to choose both *what* they see and hear about a product and also *when* they will receive this information.

## Using information to add value

Many companies use information to promote their products, and present this as an additional customer service. Such promotions are called *infomercials*, and at their best are a blend of interesting, relevant facts along with a sales pitch for the company's particular products. For example, one of the UK's largest supermarket chains sells a monthly food and home interest magazine at the sales registers in every one of their stores. Customers are so attracted to this beautifully presented magazine, filled with recipes and interesting articles about the company's own brand of products, that they pay for what is really a sales promotion. Through this highly skilled use of information, the supermarket draws new business while also adding value to the customers' shopping experience.

The Internet enables businesses to provide similar informercial services, but at considerably lower cost because sellers who make interesting information readily available tap into the Internet's culture of free exchange. The information a business offers works like an incentive gift and opens the way to building strong relationships with customers. The goodwill this fosters is of enormous benefit to word-of-mouth sales and reputation enhancement.

According to Internet marketing guru Mary Cronin (see the 'Further reading' and 'Internet addresses' sections), value-added selling differs markedly from traditional advertising: the latter sends a single, unchanging message to a wide audience, while the former provides extensive information to a select group that can choose for themselves what information they need.

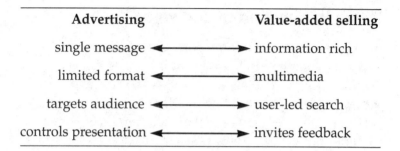

| Advertising | | Value-added selling |
|---|---|---|
| single message | ⟷ | information rich |
| limited format | ⟷ | multimedia |
| targets audience | ⟷ | user-led search |
| controls presentation | ⟷ | invites feedback |

Value-added selling can also offer a simultaneous blend of entertainment and education so that it attracts buyers by giving them novelty features and games while also maintaining their interest with useful information about products. Furthermore, unlike traditional media advertising, the Internet is forgiving. Unsuccessful promotions can be discarded or changed daily at minimum cost, which means that customer feedback can be used to improve presentations.

The main challenge for Internet sellers is to discover what kind of information their customers want and value. Here are some questions that analyse the company's current promotional activity in order to improve its contribution to overall sales results.

1   How does your business usually promote its products?

- Word of mouth?
- Printed advertisements?
- Incentive gifts?
- Other?

2   List each of your company's promotional activities and write one effective and one ineffective feature of each type of promotion.

3 Could any of the ineffective features be improved if customers were given more information?

4 What would this information be?

5 In general, what are your customers' main interests?

6 Put yourself in the place of a new buyer. What information about your products would be most interesting and useful?

7 When developing a product or service, what data do you gather as a matter of routine which may also interest your customers?

8 How can questionnaires or fact sheets be used to summarise and explain your product's special features?

9 Are there any anecdotes about the company's origins or attractive features of its work environment which customers would be interested in learning?

10 How can you present product information so that current users are interested enough to pass promotional information on to your target group?

## Analysing what works

Some recent optimistic survey results show that as many as 60% of UK businesses are planning to use the Internet for product promotion or have already begun to do so. Although this figure is likely to be an exaggeration, there *are* numerous examples of profitable business ventures launched on the Internet. Even so, this success has little impact on those firms which continue to hold back. Some of these companies simply lack the skills to begin, others are confused by the Internet's lack of structure or obvious hierarchy, and still others are unwilling to risk investing in expensive equipment and software when there seems to be no guarantee of an audience for their sales promotions. Any company still hesitating can only benefit from looking at examples of successful sales efforts as well as at some failed attempts.

*Selling successes*
Used cars

In 1985, the used-car market in Japan was transformed by an innovator who used computer networks and satellite links to organise wholesale auctions of used cars. Formerly, the cars had to be transported to locations around the country where live auctions occurred, and this resulted in an average of 65% unsold inventory. The new system requires only that photographs of the cars be taken in advance of the sale. Because the cars are located around the country, the photos allow the cars to be 'shown' electronically to buyers viewing them on computer screens. The use of this computer network enables more buyers to see more cars, eliminates the cost of transporting cars to auctions, and increases buyers' convenience. The actual location of the cars and the site of the auction become irrelevant: instead, *information* about the cars has now become the focus of attention and activity.

Delivery service

An international parcel-delivery firm uses its internal package-monitoring system to develop a new service for customers who are now able to track on their own computers the route which their packages follow while being delivered. By connecting to the delivery company's Internet site and entering their parcel's number, customers can trace their package's location, learn when it has been delivered and even 'see' who signed for it. This ability to trace a package's whereabouts sets this company apart and adds considerable value to its service. The tracking information is like an incentive gift *thrown in free* on payment of the delivery charges.

Fuel sales

A US diesel-fuel company has captured a large share of the long-haul delivery market by providing unattended automated fuel machines along the major motorways at convenient locations. Lorry drivers gain access to fuel quickly and efficiently in specially designed bays by using identification *smart cards*. Their transport-company managers are now not only able to buy fuel in bulk but can also monitor the fuel usage of individual drivers across their whole system. *High-quality automated information* about the volume, time and date of fuel usage is now readily available both for fuel purchasers to analyse their needs, and for the fuel company to use for credit-control purposes.

*'Nice Try' awards*
Publishing

An entrepreneur purchased the electronic rights to a short story written by an author whose books have sold over 150 million copies world-wide. She made an announcement to a number of electronic bulletin boards and promoted the availability of the short story on the Internet before it was to appear in print, and then asked for £3.00 from each user who wanted to see a copy by having it downloaded onto their own computers. Unfortunately, only a few dozen copies were sold. An analysis of this venture revealed a possible error in her offering copies of text in the manner of a traditional publisher. Readers who were willing to wait just a short time could buy the story in a book format at little more expense. Her advance sales idea could have worked better if she had found a way to add value to the story by providing generally unknown information about the author or an interview or anecdotes about the story's development. She needed to offer buyers *exclusive information* which the story's reader could only access by purchasing that story through the Internet.

Fast food

An international fast-food giant decided to use the Internet to promote its cuisine. It spent a fortune advertising through the conventional press and television to announce that it was going on the Internet. Its Internet site, when it was finally launched, contained a great many pictures and graphics and featured a complicated game requiring users to have a great deal of available memory if they were to use the site. Those with older computers found that the promotion was very slow to appear on their screens, and many experienced their screens 'freezing' on page one. Those who did gain full access discovered lists of nutrition information for each of the restaurant's menu items, photographs of prize-winning managers and maps of major cities which highlighted the company's restaurant locations. However, the overall consumer response was one of annoyance and complaint.

The following lists highlight those features of Internet promotions which seem to work and those which clearly do not.

*Key features of success:*

- Identifying what information customers really want to know

- Focusing on customers' convenience

- Giving an exclusive service

- Using technology to pioneer new services

- Turning information about products into a new and valued service

*Key features of failure:*

- Disregarding the customers' needs

- Annoying customers with uninteresting information

- Straining customers' equipment with poor use of technology

- Misjudging the value customers give to a product

- Failing to enhance the product with added and desired information

## Internet pros and cons

Using the Internet to promote brand recognition and
enhance a company's image through newsletters, value-
added information services and requests for customer
feedback and suggestions can lead indirectly to improved
sales. What's more, an *Internet address* is fast becoming a
signal to customers that a company is progressive and up-
to-date. Increasingly, traditional advertisements include
an Internet address beginning with 'http://www' (see
page 53) in the background. Whatever individual managers
feel about the Internet, it is now as much a part of
commercial life as the computer, and there is no going back.

Even so, some company leaders may still decide that the
Internet is of limited value to their businesses. For example,
professional firms or those companies specialising in
services rather than in retail sales or manufacturing are
very likely to see little advantage in an Internet connection.
Such companies sell know-how rather than tangible
products and are used to *chasing after* business rather than
having it 'surf' to their doorsteps – electronically or
otherwise. Nevertheless, these businesses *could* benefit from
reconsidering the way that they sell their services because
in fact they have a great deal to gain from promoting their
firms through value-added information services. For
example, solicitors and accountants can offer potential
customers updates and general advice as tax law changes,
and this approach indirectly draws *new* business when such
promotional material is made available to the right
audience (see Friday's chapter, page 73).

Deciding to use the Internet for selling requires a thorough evaluation of what company leaders wish to achieve over the long term. If this includes maintaining a contemporary image, making easy contact with potential buyers and an opportunity to learn from their customers' comments, then the Internet is not only right for the business, but essential.

## Summary

Today's chapter has examined how the Internet is different from all other advertising media and highlighted those features of Internet promotion which succeed. This provides a background for tomorrow's discussion of the World Wide Web.

# The World Wide Web

Consumer expectations for Internet images can be high, and although technical advances have been rapid, there is still a wide gap between television-image quality and the quality of computer images. This is frustrating for those who want to offer exciting Internet promotions, and yet these limitations are actually beneficial because they force sellers to consider the differences between the Internet and other media.

One promotional advantage of printed advertisements and television and radio commercials is their appearance *alongside* entertainment, news and other features. On the other hand, the Internet sales promotions have to be interesting enough to attract attention *without* the help of other accompanying features. A 'flashy' approach is not necessarily the way to achieve this, and today's chapter explains why. Starting with a description of the World Wide Web, it highlights the importance of presenting a consistent message and then describes how the Internet enables direct contact with customers to be made. Topics include:

- Defining the World Wide Web
- Presenting a clear message
- Interaction with customers

## Defining the World Wide Web

The World Wide Web (WWW) is only one of many ways to use the Internet for communication, but it is fast becoming the most popular. Therefore, understanding how it works and its relationship to the Internet is essential for the development of an effective sales strategy.

The Web is made up of a collection of documents each of which is called a *home page* or *site*. All of these pages are produced by using the same computer code – called Hypertext Markup Language (HTML) – which gives each document a uniform format. Alternatively, the Internet is an international network of cables, wiring and user connections through which home pages are transmitted and made accessible.

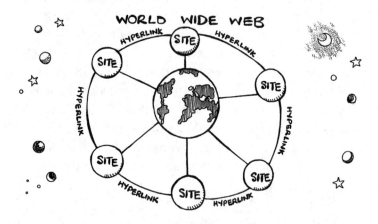

Included in each home page are *hyperlinks*, that is, key words, symbols or phrases which are reference points to other parts of the same document or to other documents also on the Web. Users indicate an interest in seeing one of these other sections by using either a keyboard or a mouse to highlight the hyperlink. They can then jump directly to the new material. Jumping from link to link allows users to choose both what they see and the order in which they wish to see it. Home-page documents can be stored anywhere in the world, and it takes the same amount of time to jump to a page in Bangkok as it does to jump to one in Paris. The ability to connect in this way is one of the Web's main attractions, and it also lends itself to browsing so that a user may start with a home page featuring alternative rock music and end up looking at a page describing the merits of an insurance policy.

Here is a definition for the World Wide Web:

> The World Wide Web is a collection of documents which are produced using a single computer code. Each of these contains hyperlinks which allow users to move from one document to another. Potentially, every document is linked to all of the others.

It is possible for a home page to include links to any other home page also accessible on the Web. This is due to the Internet's addressing or labelling standard, called Uniform Resource Locator (URL). Every home page on the Web also has a standardised address which begins with 'http://www'. This stands for 'hypertext transfer protocol:// world wide web', and refers to the code a computer uses in order to send and receive Web documents using the Internet system. Currently, there are software vendors tinkering with the HTML code and others proposing to transform HTML into a more complex computer language. Improvement and change are inevitable, but generally there is a recognition among Web developers that coordination and a common standard are necessary. The group responsible for setting, developing

and improving WWW standards is the World Wide Web
Consortium (see the 'Internet addresses' section). This is a
collaborative effort based in both Europe and the US.
Although it is funded by industry, the software and
products it develops are made available, free of charge, to
all.

*Hypertext Markup Language*
HTML was invented in 1965 by Ted Nelson who described
it as *nonsequential writing*. It is text which includes
**highlighted** or <u>underlined</u> references to other text. The
*hypertext* is the additional reading material which is
accessed by using the highlighted references or hyperlinks.
A single-page document written in HTML can include
several links to other Web documents so that it becomes
enriched through its hypertext connections. Home-page
developers can add depth to their documents and benefit
their users when their hyperlinks are well-chosen. Anyone
who has ever used a computer 'help' file has experienced
using a form of HTML.

*The Web's origins*
In 1989 Tim Berners-Lee, an Englishman working at the
Conseil Européen pour la Recherche Nucleaire (CERN) in
Switzerland, used HTML to make research data more easily
accessible to his colleagues. His idea was to use hyperlinks
to connect related research documents so that users could
instantaneously access data stored within other networks
located around the world. The obvious advantages of
connecting related files in this way quickly led to a
widespread acceptance of the idea first within CERN and
then within the general international scientific community.

Gradually, this interest spread further to other users, and in 1992, CERN made the coding for producing Web pages widely available to those outside of the academic and research communities. Along with others, they also provided methods to catalogue, organise and search through Web pages. Enthusiasm led to further enthusiasm, so that the Web has now become, in the words of Tim Berners-Lee: 'a universe of network-accessible information' (see *Hypertext Online Style Guide*, in the 'Internet addresses' section).

*Do-it-yourself issues*
The HTML code itself is straightforward so that skilled computer users can pick up the basics in as little as three hours. Those who are less skilled, on the other hand, need to be realistic. If they don't already understand computer jargon, they will have difficulty following even *easy to learn* style instructions, and this will mean several days of experimenting and reading before a home page can be developed. Even then, the page may include errors and should be thoroughly tested before being launched as a Web site. Producing a Web page in-house without either design or technical advisers is certainly a possibility, and it will do no harm for decision-makers to learn the basics of page production. However, if the end result looks amateurish or includes links which do not work, then it is time to call in the professionals. The company's business image is on the line, and a good result is necessary if the page is intended to generate sales.

Further help is on the way for those who wish to explore home page development for themselves because new software programs are now being offered which bypass the need to learn HTML or any other programming code. These programs allow page developers to produce home pages by typing in commands similar to those which enable word-processor users to add highlights, italics and other desktop publishing features. This makes *do-it-yourself* a more viable alternative.

## Presenting a clear message

Consistency is a selling essential: a business needs to present a clear, consistent message to its buyers throughout all of its promotional efforts, including those it develops for the Internet. This requires *more* than developing a home page which uses a similar style and layout to a company's printed brochures and stationery. It means that the way the company presents itself on the Internet should be in line with its overall goals and in harmony with its brand image. Tuesday's chapter included a description of a fast-food chain's home page which was widely criticised, forcing the company to reinvent its Internet image. Essentially, the page was both *over-* and *under-*ambitious because it tried to achieve a variety of different objectives by patching together mismatched pieces of information, but made no attempt to express any overall corporate values. Again and again, buyers are attracted to products which are promoted with integrity. When sellers are clear about what they want to achieve, they make more effective decisions about all of their promotional activities. The temptation is always to be all things to all people, but it is a better course to focus on what really matters to the company and then present that in an attractive manner.

## Know your audience

The GVU Center's survey data (see page 16) presents a profile of users who are well-educated and well-paid. More informal surveys reveal them also to be people who are less interested in traditionally packaged commercials. This is good news because, as mentioned before, computer images are as yet unable to compete with television-picture quality. Internet users want information about products available, ways to use them, what they are made of and how they work. They want to see them in relation to other products, and to be able to make comments to the people who sell them. When promotions meet these requirements, bells, whistles and dancing elephants become unnecessary.

## The staff review

Before the page is launched, it should be viewed by staff from a variety of backgrounds, including both skilled and unskilled Internet users. This approach saves embarrassment. The home page of one leading UK retailer was recently reviewed in the national press and described as surprisingly awful, with the reviewer adding that the company had ample resources to do even a little better.

This situation could have been avoided if the site had been reviewed by staff and tested, so that it was improved before any outsiders saw it.

It is surprising that any developers ignore this need because changes to design and content can be made with relative ease: pages can be altered on a daily basis if staff feedback indicates that errors have been made. If the sales objectives of the site are defined in advance, then the results of an in-house review can be very revealing when staff reactions are compared against the original objectives. If there is less than an 80% approval rate or, alternatively, less than a 60% match between the staff's reactions and the original objectives, then the promotion needs significant revision. The following list of questions helps to evaluate the contents of a home page:

*Evaluating a home page*
1  Is the overall tone positive and in line with the company's values and ideas?

2  Is there a clear connection between what the company has to offer and any information service being presented on the page?

3  Are any games that are included actually fun to play?

4  Are customers likely to be interested in any of the facts, graphs and charts that are included?

5  Are the references (i.e. hyperlinks) to other parts of the site likely to interest customers? Are there any alternative ideas for hyperlink connections to additional site features?

## Interaction with customers

The Web makes communication with customers both direct and inexpensive. Through home pages, companies can ask for reactions to their products and also offer detailed information with greater precision. There are now data-management programs which recognise repeat visitors to a site, greet them by name and ask them the equivalent of 'Do you want the usual?' This kind of service, however, requires high-powered computers with a considerable memory capacity for storing customer data and preferences, and so it is not a solution for everyone.

The commercial attitude behind the service, nonetheless, *can* benefit every business. At its heart is the belief that customers who feel recognised, valued and served are more likely to be loyal to the brand than those who don't. Home-page promotion at its best can bring a *more* personal approach to selling. Developers need to anticipate what their customers want to know and then choose words or symbols as hyperlinks which *anyone* can understand. Simplicity is the best approach here since it will help ordinary users to feel that the page has been designed with *their* needs, not those of a robot, in mind.

To give one example, a supplier of automotive parts used home-page technology to reduce dramatically its number of order mistakes. Formerly, customers telephoned or faxed their orders by using the company's thick catalogue, or by describing the part they needed to the sales clerk taking the order. Errors were easily made with this system because the catalogue's print was small, and guesswork was often needed to decide part sizes. However, the company has now produced an electronic brochure with a full range of automotive parts available for customers to review on screen.

*How it works*
In the above example, the purchasing process starts when the customer contacts the company's database through an Internet connection and then types in the brand name and model number of the car. The computer then offers a menu of choices, including engine, body, electrical and interior parts. As each selection is made, further categories are offered so that the customer gradually narrows the field down to a specific part. It can take as few as four screens or as many as twenty to find the right part – in either case, customers appreciate the convenience, removal of guesswork and ease of selection involved. Once the final choices are made, the part's order numbers and other information are automatically entered onto an order form,

and invoices are then based on this order. Errors throughout the whole process are minimised.

Although this solution required an initial investment, it has more than paid for itself through increased sales and word-of-mouth promotion from satisfied customers. When Internet selling is thus organised so that its unique benefits are used, it offers a significant improvement in convenience for customers.

## Summary

Today's chapter has presented the World Wide Web as the primary means for promoting sales on the Internet and offered criteria for creating successful sites. Tomorrow's chapter will explore the steps to home page development.

# Developing a home page

These are the Internet's pioneering days, and although users' expectations can be high, they also enjoy simpler efforts if these have style and something worthwhile to offer. Therefore, the choice of content is as important as design and technical skills when developing a site. Home pages produced with this point in mind are more likely to attract users who not only enjoy the site but also tell others about it. Developers also need to be aware that the site will be accessed by an international audience, and so language differences have to be taken into account as well.

Today's chapter focuses on the practical issues involved in creating a home page for business promotion, and examines the steps involved in home-page design: deciding and organising the content, planning the layout, choosing hyperlinks and writing and testing the HTML code. It also

presents the benefits of including electronic forms for
information-gathering. The topics are:

- Five steps to a home page

- Getting feedback from customers

## Five steps to a home page

Developing a home page is a complex task, and the
'Further reading' section suggests excellent books which go
into this subject in detail. The five steps presented here
highlight essential stages of this process and provide an
overview of what is required. The five steps are:

- deciding what to include

- organising the content

- planning the layout

- choosing the hyperlinks

- writing and testing the HTML code

*Deciding what to include*
The first step requires selecting what company and product
information should be included. Company leaders need to
check the content of the home page themselves even if they
have hired a specialist designer, and this should be done
before any technical decisions are made. This ensures that
the content is in line with the company's overall marketing
plans. The following questions focus on the issues which
need attention:

1 What products should be promoted, and how should they be described?

2 What company information should be highlighted?

3 Is there a value-added service or entertainment feature which can be offered?

4 What pictures, graphics, colours and sounds suit your company best?

5 What degree of interaction with customers is appropriate?

6 What methods can be used to gather customer comments?

The information which can be included in a home page is limited to the computer memory available for storing it. In particular, if a home page 'lives' in a service provider's memory, then the rental charges for memory need to be considered. A home page with several photos, graphics, animation and sound requires a great deal of memory. Each section should therefore be brief and to the point so that it requires as few screens as possible. A *screen* refers to the amount of information that fits onto a computer screen. Long sections require users to scroll through many screens in order to find what they need, and this can be hard on the eyes. Also, home pages are viewed by an international audience whose knowledge of English may be limited. As a courtesy, complex language and multi-screened sections should therefore be avoided.

*Organising the content*

The second step to home page development requires grouping this information into smaller sections and deciding how each of these fit together logically. This step establishes a basic design and also leads to identifying which words or phrases should be used as the hyperlinks to connect each of the sections to each other. The following are questions which help in this decision-making:

1  What is the main message your company wants to convey about its business overall?

2  What text, pictures and sounds convey this message most clearly?

3  What other information supports this main message?

4  How can this supporting information be clustered into subgroups?

5  How can each subgroup be labelled so that its heading clearly describes its contents?

6  How do each of the subgroups relate to each other?

*Planning the layout*

The third step requires developers to plan how each section of the page can be connected to each other section. It is helpful to use pieces of paper in order to represent these planned connections because a visual demonstration reveals oversights and errors in advance and contributes to a logical and pleasing design. Although this step begins to move into technical areas, it is valuable for non-technical managers to take part in this stage of the process as well. Specialist designers or those with a strong engineering bias cannot really distinguish, on a company's behalf, between what is crucial and significant information and what is just supporting data. The final layout can be left to the experts, but a rough draft should be examined by those responsible for the business. Tim Berners-Lee, in his *Hypertext Online Style Guide* (see the 'Internet addresses' section), suggests that any document five pages or longer should be linked in sequence as a *string*. Here are directions for this kind of layout:

1   List the headings given to each of the subgroups on a single sheet of paper, and lay this on a large empty surface. This represents the home page *cover sheet* – also called its *table of contents*.

2   Then, write the names of each of these headings on separate sheets of paper.

3   Place these sheets on the surface, and arrange them so that they show a logical sequence or progression from one topic to another.

4   Keeping to that sequence, organise them in relation to the cover sheet illustrated as in the diagram opposite.

This basic design allows users to jump from each section directly to the cover page, or alternatively to move from section to section in sequence. Section hyperlinks can be represented by icons of buttons at the top of each screen saying 'start', 'next', and 'previous'.

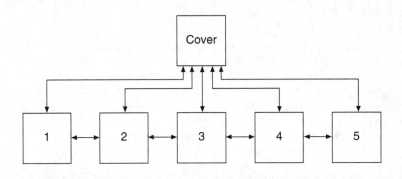

5   Another layout format is the *outline*. An outline format is useful when a seller knows that visitors to the site have different interests and information needs. It is also useful when the home page has several distinct sections, such as company history, personnel information and descriptions of company products.

To develop the outline format, you can use the same sheets of paper and rearrange them so that each of the separate sections are clustered into general subject categories. This layout may need the addition of new sheets to expand the outline. Number each sheet, as illustrated in the diagram, as a reminder of the sequence to be used. Each sheet needs a link to the cover sheet –

'start', – with words from the text then used to provide links to other sections.

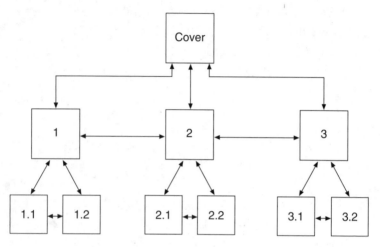

It is possible to include links for both sequence and outline layouts, as well as for other layouts within the same home page design. Although this is a complex project for developers, it is unlikely to confuse users because they would only see the hyperlinks not the layouts which underlie them.

### Choosing the hyperlinks

As described in Wednesday's chapter, hyperlinks are the words, phrases or symbols within a document which serve as reference points or links to other parts of the same document or even to other World Wide Web pages. They are the features which give users the freedom to move at will throughout the Web. After deciding the home page layout, developers should return to the content of each section in their document. They may need to edit this material so that it includes appropriate words which can serve as hyperlinks. It helps users to remember which parts of the document they have already seen if the hyperlinks are coded so that they change colour, or are highlighted in some way, once they have been used.

*Writing and testing the HTML code*
This topic requires in-depth study. The list of suggestions which follow offer positive additions to the development of any home page.

Remember:

- Include the home page Uniform Resource Locator (URL), that is its address, on every page. This is a courtesy to users who may print only one section of the home page and forget to make a note of its address
- Because some users enter a site from links on a different home page entirely, every section should have a link back to the site's own table of contents
- Design the page so that those users whose software allows them to access text only can still benefit from the page. An overdependence on colour and graphics automatically limits the page to users with high-speed, top-of-the-line equipment
- Include a 'mail to:' hyperlink within the document to encourage customer response. This is an alternative to listing the company's e-mail address, and makes it easier for customers to make contact with the company
- Use a uniform and consistent presentation style from section to section. This simplifies the page and makes a better overall impression

- Include navigational signals such as 'back,' 'forward', 'start' and 'exit' in case users do not have software which enables them to control their movements while visiting a page
- Provide an index of all hyperlinks included within the page which change colour or become highlighted after the sections that they refer to have been seen
- Test the page thoroughly before launching it on the Web, using all of the better-known software programs designed for browsing through Web sites. Ask colleagues with little computer experience to test the hyperlinks: if *they* can use the page, then potential customers are unlikely to have any problems
- Review the home page regularly to ensure both that each of its links continues to work and is free of error messages, and that any links to other home pages continue to function properly

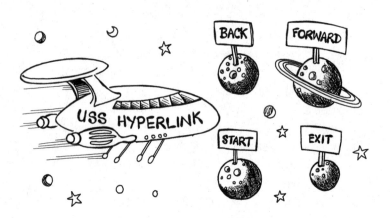

## Getting feedback from customers

HTML makes it possible to include electronic forms which can be completed by home page users. This feature is extremely valuable for the following reasons:

*Benefits of electronic forms:*

- Client information is readily added to the company's database

- Questions can be chosen in order to gather specific data

- Product preferences can be easily analysed

- It is a low-cost method for conducting customer surveys

Two issues need to be addressed in order to ensure that electronic forms will work. First, page developers should contact their service provider (or consult their in-house engineers if the company has its own backbone connection) and ask if the computer which stores the Web page has Computer Gateway Interface (CGI) capability. This is a program which enables the server computer to record the answers given by users as they complete a form. If a home page is managed by a computer without CGI capability, users will get error messages, beeps or other uniquely annoying computer signals when they try to complete a form. Even if a page is beautifully designed, if it offers a form which doesn't work, then users will be unhappy. Another problem for users arises if they do not have the kind of communications software which allows them to fill in forms as they view the home page.

The solution for both of these issues is to include specific directions for users to transfer the form to their own computers using a feature called a File Transfer Protocol (FTP) address. After they transfer the form to their own computer, they can complete it by using their own computer's word processing program and then send it by e-mail to the company. This solution also applies to *Guest Book* features which invite users to add their names and addresses to the company's database. Alternatively, a 'mail to' hyperlink can be included on the page. This link leads to an e-mail message screen so that users can type in any comments, requests for information or data they wish.

## Summary

Today's chapter has addressed the stages to home page development and emphasised the importance of making it easy for customers to give feedback. Tomorrow's chapter will focus on methods and tools to attract the customer.

# Getting customers' attention

The most imaginative, well-designed and information-rich Web page is completely useless unless potential customers know how to find it. Therefore, telling users about the site is very important. It is also the subject of today's chapter, which looks at: understanding what *browsers* are and how they work; identifying which *search engines* are most likely to be used by desirable buyers; assessing the merits of Internet *shopping malls*; and forming and using alliances for mutual gain. A final topic highlights the need to respect the Internet's unique code of conduct, called *netiquette*. Features of this code are presented together with a discussion of the benefits it brings to a successful sales campaign. Topics thus include:

- Browsing with purpose
- Searching through the Web
- Cybermalls and piggyback selling
- Internet soft sell

## Browsing with purpose

A successful sales promotion of any kind depends upon attracting the attention of desirable buyers. This means first identifying a suitable audience and then discovering how best to reach it. Because the Internet is growing and changing daily, it is particularly challenging to discover the most productive way to contact customers. There is a gold-rush mentality among sellers, who are in a hurry to promote their products and who hold the belief that buyers will simply appear. In theory, site promotion should be easy – after all, everyone is connected to everyone else on the Web – but in practice, it is very difficult indeed. The main challenge is the lack of any proven methods for success. This is both good and bad news: good because everyone gets to invent a whole new way of attracting customers, and bad for the very same reason, because after a frustrating session at the computer screen, it would be nice to discover that there *is* a rule book after all.

*What is a browser?*
When the Internet first began to grow, its pioneering users realised that the wealth of information available to them needed to be organised so that they could find data when they wanted it. *Browsers* are the software programs developed to conduct these searches. It is their task to sift through thousands and thousands of files taken from a world filled with different databases in order to find the information which users request. Browsers enable users to visit sites; transmit the contents they find to their own screens; and then save those files that they wish to review later. They are designed to make Internet access easy and

efficient, and also to locate sites when users do not have a specific URL address.

*How do browsers work?*
Browsers are stored either in the users' computer or with their service provider. They begin to work after either a telephone or a leased line Internet connection is made and the user activates the browser by typing an address, clicking a mouse or striking a key. Each browser has its own style of introducing itself, but they all provide a space into which the user types a name, address or subject heading. Service provider helplines, introductory Internet guides and Internet magazines (see the 'Further reading' section) offer detailed advice on using browsers effectively. It is beneficial for sellers to understand this process because it is what their potential customers have to carry out in order to visit their sites: browsers bring the sites to the users' screens.

The following is a partial list of popular browsers which are used by an international audience.

Lynx

This is a text-only browser, which means that it hasn't got the ability to bring graphics and photographs to the users' screens: any non-text features included in a file will show up on the screen as blank space. For example, it is possible to use the Internet to visit some of the world's great art galleries. Although Lynx does allow a user to read any *text material* stored in the document, it cannot show the pictures. Many older computers have low levels of memory and power, and therefore are limited to using text-only browsers. Web page developers should consider this when designing their home pages.

## Mosaic

This is probably the most frequently used browser in the world. It was designed by Marc Andreessen when he worked at the US National Center for Supercomputer Applications (NCSA), and there are many versions available. Mosaic made an important contribution to the Web because it was the first browser with the ability to transmit colour and graphics. This opened the way for colourful, dynamic Web page presentations.

## Netscape

This is an advanced browser also developed by Marc Andreessen. Not only does this browser transmit colour, graphics and sound, but users can read text and move around the page while pictures and other features are still being copied by the browser. This makes visiting home pages less frustrating. Users can visit the site, read its index and essential text information and decide to leave before the full-colour photo of the company's managing director has had a chance to appear Cheshire-cat-like on the screen.

## Internet Explorer

The software giant, Microsoft, only recently became interested in the Internet. It promotes its browser as Netscape's main rival, and it does offer several good features with promised improvements to come at an unspecified date in the future. Microsoft's attitude towards its customers will ultimately determine its ability to compete with Netscape.

## Searching through the Web

As the number of Web sites began to increase dramatically, individuals and groups started making Web *index pages*. These are lists of Web sites which are organised according to subject. Users in search of information are able to visit an index page (having arrived there through using their browser) and type in key words which describe the subject they want. This request results in a list of all the Web pages available in that index which refer to the requested subject. These index pages are also called *search engines*, and they are rapidly becoming the first port of call for users for either business or leisure purposes. In order for companies to be assured of entry into an index, page developers should contact the index organisers directly. A listing in prominent search engines is crucial in order to draw users to a site.

*Choosing key words*

Each search engine operates independently and has its own process for companies to apply for entry to the list, but they all have in common the need for page developers to choose key words which describe the subjects that their home pages address. These words categorise the page and determine in which sections of the index it is to be listed. This may seem easy but it actually requires understanding how site visitors are likely to describe a product or service when they first launch their search. The most active search engines have *robots* or *spiders*, that is, automatic programs which trawl throughout the Web reading home-page titles and section headings so that they can add any new items they find to their index. This means that references to home pages may be included in an index without any effort made by their developers if the pages have been designed with indexing in mind.

*Getting listed*

One way to gain immediate attention from search engine users is to buy advertising space in the opening pages of an index, but this can be an expensive option. At the time of writing, it costs £500 per month for inclusion in Yahoo's (see below) launch feature. Unfortunately, because this kind of service is so new, it is not certain what kind of return there is for this fee. The real task is to get a site listed in as many indexes as possible and then update these listings regularly, especially if new features have been added to the page. A company called *Submit It* (see the 'Internet addresses' section) offers to list a site in 15 different indexes without charge.

### Popular search engines

Sellers should research which search engines are most likely to be used by the audience they want to reach. Here are some helpful questions to ask search engine organisers who charge fees for including a home page in their index. A list of popular search engines then follows.

> * Does the index specialise in any subjects?
> * What subjects or categories are visited most frequently?
> * Is the index a commercial venture, or is it an educational project?
> * How is the index updated, and how frequently?

*SavySearch (http://www.cs.colostate.edu)*

This search engine searches through 13 of the most popular search engine files – including Yahoo, Lycos and others – simultaneously. Users need only enter a key word once, and this gets the whole process underway. An enormously time-saving facility.

*Yahoo (http://www.yahoo.com)*

One of the biggest and best, say many reviewers. It has a very active index system for updating its entries.

*Web Crawler (http://www.webcrawler.com)*

This search engine is kept up-to-date by conducting automatic searches in the Web for new sites. It accepts as many as 13 million search requests per week.

*Lycos (http:www.lycos.com)*

This has thousands of entries and a high success rate for searches.

*Yellow Pages (http://www.ncp.com)*

This index is growing fast and receiving excellent reviews. If sellers want to develop a market in the USA, then getting a listing in this index is essential.

*World Wide Web Worm (http://128.138.236.18/home/mcbryan)*

This index includes 3 million Web addresses and is used by more than 2 million people each month. It offers a staggering amount of information.

*Excite (http://www.excite.com)*

This index offers reviews of Web sites, with hyperlinks to the sites it lists. It receives very positive reviews.

*The Whole Internet Catalog (http://www.nearnet.gnn.com)*

This index is the on-line version of Ed Krol's highly praised book *The Whole Internet* (see the 'Further reading' section). Anyone who reads this best-selling book is very likely to want to search in this index.

## Cybermalls and piggyback selling

An increasingly popular way in which users begin browsing in the Web is by visiting an Internet shopping mall – a *cybermall*. On paper, this is a list of businesses which have developed home pages and added hyperlinks to each others' sites as well as to an introductory page for the mall. On screen, it is a world of colour, sound, graphics and text which enable users to buy products and view special offers as if they were really in a shop. This is a form of *piggyback selling* because users may first visit the mall in order to view one of its shops and then be attracted to other shops and make impulse purchases.

Britain's largest cybermall, BarclaySquare (see the 'Internet addresses' section), is a shopping service organised by Barclays Bank. It has 14 shops, at the time of writing, including Interflora and Sainsbury's, and users can order products directly from its shops using credit cards, with transactions encrypted and processed through Barclays Bank. The popularity of this site has far exceeded its developers' expectations: during its first 10 months of operation, it logged almost 1.5 million requests to visit shops within the mall.

US cybermalls show an even greater degree of popularity. In April 1995, the Internet Shopping Network (see the 'Internet addresses' section) launched a mall offering 20,000 products. This was the first and most visible Internet mass purchasing project, and it is now believed to be one of the most popular Web sites, with 25% of its revenue coming from outside the US. The site was purchased after its first six months by the US cable-television sales specialists, the Home Shopping Network, for £3.3 million.

## Internet soft sell

There are certain sites on the Internet which are put aside for discussion only. These may be called forums, conferences or chat or discussion groups, and they are usually managed by a volunteer moderator who is called a *systems operator* or *sysop*. People who are so enthusiastic about selling their products that they ignore all resistance need to be aware that there are restrictions on using some forms of discussion group for business. Participants in groups with primarily social functions do not take kindly to having their screen space invaded by sales promotions. Even in those discussion groups formed so that members can announce business opportunities, there are certain subtle rules of behaviour. These are posted in an FAQ file – which stands for *frequently asked questions* – and newcomers to discussion groups are expected to read this file before participation. If a user doesn't know how to gain access to this file, it is acceptable to post a short notice asking for this information.

Those who ignore these formalities can find themselves being *flamed*, that is deluged with angry e-mail messages from around the world. *Flame wars*, as they are called, can clog up a service provider's system, so that guilty parties can lose their account. It is therefore better to be safe than sorry and work to improve, not destroy, an Internet business image.

*An alternative approach*
An alternative approach is for a seller to join a discussion group which is related to the particular product or service being sold. As members of the group, sellers learn what potential customers want and need. They can also offer advice and answer any specialist questions so that they create an impression of expertise. Potential buyers tend to visit those sites whose developers are knowledgeable and genuinely helpful. Soft sell depends upon resisting the urge to announce special offers, and means investing time and energy into the group. It can be a very beneficial approach for long-term image-building, however, because Internet culture rewards information generosity.

## Summary

Today's chapter has highlighted the importance of designing home pages that benefit all users regardless of their browser. It has also presented the importance of search engine listings and soft sell approaches. Tomorrow's chapter is a review of the key points raised throughout the week's activities.

# Planning for action

The final step in this week-long programme is to plan what actions need to be taken in order to sell successfully on the Internet. The topics presented on each day have highlighted different features of Internet selling. These include: recognising who uses the Internet; making decisions about technology; identifying the Internet's unique benefits; exploring the World Wide Web; developing a promotional site; and examining how to attract customers to it. The following sections suggest specific activities that will put into practice the ideas presented throughout this programme.

## Sunday

1 Examine the data from Mark Lotter's surveys and the GVU Center study to identify potential customer groups.

2 Look over your answers to the questionnaire in the section'Is Internet selling for you?' (see page 17).

3 Refer to every 'No' and 'Maybe' answer and ask how you can change these to 'Yes'.

4 Research the costs of renting an ISDN line and a leased line.

5 Contact your computer supplier and ask for information about server computers – that is – routers, bridges and hubs.

## Monday

1  In terms of sales, ask where your company is now and where you want it to be in the future.

2  Refer to the three levels of investment commitment shown on page 25, and decide which level is right for your company.

3  Consider the suggestions made in the 'Decision-making essentials' section (see pages 35–7) and identify your company's specific needs.

4  Consult pricing information for leased lines, ISDN lines and computer equipment, and make decisions about new purchases.

5  Contact service providers, and decide where to open an account.

## Tuesday

1  Refer to the services that an Internet connection provides (see page 39) and consider what each offers your company.

2  Review your answers to the promotion-analysis questionnaire (see page 42).

3  Clarify further what information can be used to provide a value-added service.

4  Analyse your ideas in terms of the key features listed on pages 48–9.

5  Determine how you can develop your ideas so that you ensure success.

## Wednesday

1  Subscribe to an Internet magazine (see the 'Further reading' section) and read the home page reviews.

2  Visit a variety of sites, and decide which features you value.

3  Clarify the message you want to convey about your company through your home page.

4  Decide what kind of feedback you want from customers.

5  Identify how your home page could make purchasing easier for customers.

## Thursday

1  Decide what content you want to include in the home page, including any value-added features.

2  Organise this into a layout format.

3  Put yourself in your customers' position, and read the content carefully to identify sensible hyperlinks.

4  Realistically assess your ability to create your home page. If hesitant, begin calling professionals for quotations.

5  Determine how you want to collect feedback from customers and what you will do with it.

## Friday

1 Choose a browser: either through your service provider or by direct purchase yourself.

2 Practise using this so that you understand what your customers have to do in order to visit your site.

3 Contact all the search engines listed on pages 79–80.

4 Use a search engine to locate and visit cybermalls.

5 Explore the world of bulletin boards and news groups to discover more about who is out there using the Internet.

To conclude the week's programme, the Internet offers everyone in sales a clean piece of paper, unblemished snow and the beginning of a new day, all through emphasising qualities of creativity, invention and flexibility. Those who are truly interested in listening to their customers now have a new way to do this and a powerful means to generate success through improved communication.

# ■ INTERNET ADDRESSES ■

| | |
|---|---|
| BarclaySquare | http://www.itl.net/barclaysquare |
| BTnet | http://www.bt.net |
| CIX  Internet Service Provider | http://www.sales@compulink.co.uk |
| Mary J. Cronin | http://www.novalink.com |
| EUnet Communications | http://www.EU.net |
| GVU Center | http://www.cc.gatech.edu/gvu/user_surveys |
| *Hypertext Online Style Guide* | http://www.w3.org/hypertext/www/style |
| Internet Shopping Network | http://www.internet.net |
| Internet Society | http://www.isoc.org |
| Network Wizards | http://www.nw.com |
| Lynx | http://www.lynx.net |
| NCSA Mosaic | http://www.ncsa.uiuc.edu |
| Netscape Navigator | http://home.netscape.com |
| Submit It | http://www.submit-it.com |
| Unipalm PIPEX | http://www.ws.pipex.com |
| Vision in Practice Ltd/ Carol A. O'Connor | http://www.visiprac.com |
| World Wide Web Consortium | http://www.w3.org |

# AUTHOR'S RECOMMENDATIONS

*Modem*
Motorola 3400, 28.8 bps. Robust design and adapter plugs are also included. The company offers an excellent helpline service.

*Internet magazine*
NetUser magazine. Published monthly. Comprehensive, knowledgeable and creative.

*Browser software*
Netscape Version 2.0. A superlative browser. Versions are available free on the Internet, but purchase provides support and an advice line.

*Virus-protection software:*
Dr Solomon's Anti-Virus Toolkit. New diskettes are sent quarterly for re-installation of the program so that registered users have ongoing protection from the most current viruses.

*Web page design software*
HoTMetaL PRO 3.0. This program enables users familiar with Windows and Macintosh to make sophisticated home pages.

*Server computers*
Compaq Proliant 1500 has two Pentium chips, 32 to 250 RAM and a hard drive with 21 to 301 gigabytes.

Apple Mac 8550 has 24 megabytes of RAM and powerful add on hard drive capacity.

# ■ FURTHER READING ■

## Books

Bride, Mac, *Teach Yourself HTML*. London: Hodder & Stoughton, 1996.

Cronin, Mary J., *Doing More Business on the Internet*. International Thomson Publishing, 1995.

Gilster, Paul, *The New Internet Navigator*. John Wiley & Sons, 1995.

Janal, Daniel S., *Online Marketing Handbook*. International Thomson Publishing, 1995.

Krol, Ed, *The Whole Internet User's Guide and Catalog* (2nd edition). O'Reilly & Associates, 1994.

Resnick, Rosalind and Taylor, David, *The Internet Business Guide*. Sams Publishing, 1994.

Sterne, Jim, *World Wide Web Marketing: Integrating the Internet into Your Marketing Strategy*. John Wiley & Sons, 1995.

Young, Margaret Levine and Levine, John R., *Internet FAQ's*. IDG Books Worldwide, 1995.

## Recommended Internet magazine

*NetUser Magazine*. Paragon Publishing Ltd, Paragon House, St Peter's Road, Bournemouth, BH1 2JS, England.

*backbone*
super-powerful lines belonging to governments,
universities and industry which enable separate computer
networks to connect and work together as the Internet

*bandwidth*
the capacity of a cable or electronic line to carry data at
speed: the higher the bandwidth, the greater the capacity

*browsers*
software programs which are developed to conduct
searches through files stored on the Internet

*CERN* (Conseil Européen pour la Recherche Nucleaire)
a research facility in Switzerland where in 1989 Tim
Berners-Lee first used hypertext markup language (see
later) to connect research data from around the world

*Computer Gateway Interface (CGI)*
a program which enables users to answer questionnaires
and surveys and make direct contact with sellers on the
World Wide Web

*cyberspace*
a term coined by science fiction writer, William Gibson,
which refers to the 'world' created by computer images and
electronic connections

*cybermall*
an Internet shopping mall formed by several sellers in
order to promote their products and services together.
Visitors to one seller's site have access to the other sellers'
products and services

*e-mail* (also *electronic mail*)
a method of sending messages by way of the Internet from
one computer to another

*FAQ files*
lists of *frequently asked questions* from new users to an
Internet chat, discussion, conference or bulletin board
group. The answers provide an orientation for getting the
most from joining the group and avoiding giving offence

*File Transfer Protocol (FTP)*
a program allowing users to transfer files stored in another
computer to their own computer

*flame wars*
result from giving offence on the Internet so that users
deluge each other with e-mail messages and cause each
other's systems to become clogged

*gateways*
entry points to the Internet backbone system through very
powerful computers

*Guest Book*
a feature which enables users to leave their name and
e-mail address to be entered onto a seller's database

*hit*
the record of a user's visit to a home page

*home page* (also *site*)
a document produced by using HTML code (see below)
with links to the World Wide Web. It is developed by
individual users for their own unique purposes

*hypertext markup language (HTML)*
text which includes references to additional reading
material. The references, called hyperlinks, are highlighted
and users gain access to this additional material by clicking
a mouse or using the keyboard

*hyperlinks*
key words, symbols or phrases which provide links to other parts of the same  document or to other documents written in HTML code (see previous entry)

*Information Superhighway*
a term used to describe the Internet referring to the way that information is *routed* rapidly around the world electronically

*Internet*
an electronic network made up of other independent networks located around the world.  It offers a common means to share information and provide services

*Internet Address* (see *Uniform Resource Locator*)

*Internet Service Providers*
commercial organisations which offer users with less powerful computers an entry point to high speed Internet lines

*Internet Society*
promotes the Internet's evolution by offering education and technology support and by providing a forum for developing new Internet applications

*netiquette*
standards of behaviour which contribute to courteous use of the Internet

*network*
a system or chain of interconnected computers which work together

*search engines*
sophisticated indexing services which organise lists of home pages according to subject

*site* (see *home page)*

*System Access Providers*
commercial organisations which offer direct access to the
Internet's backbone system requiring significant investment
in leased lines and equipment by clients

*systems operator* (also *sysop)*
a volunteer moderator of a discussion, chat, conference or
bulletin board group responsible for maintaining the
group's agreed standards

*Uniform Resource Locator (URL)*
an Internet address. World Wide Web addresses begin with
*http://www.*

*value added selling*
an approach to selling which offers special benefits to
buyers enhancing the purchased product or service

*virtual reality*
an electronic arena created by software programs and
computer generated images: highly realistic, but entirely
intangible

*World Wide Web (WWW)*
a collection of documents which are produced by using a
single computer code called hypertext markup language
(see earlier) so that each document can be connected to any
other document also written in this code

*World Wide Web Consortium*
brings together experts from leading computer and
software companies, internationally renowned computer
laboratories and members of other Internet task force
teams; provides common standards for developing the
World Wide Web

**Further** *Successful Business in a Week* **titles from** Hodder & Stoughton and the Institute of Management all at £5.99

| 0 340 59856 5 | Finance for Non-Financial Managers ❐ | 0 340 57522 0 | Successful Motivation ❐ |
|---|---|---|---|
| 0 340 63152 X | Introducing Management ❐ | 0 340 55538 6 | Successful Negotiating ❐ |
| 0 340 62742 5 | Introduction to Bookkeeping | 0 340 64341 2 | Successful Networking ❐ |
| | and Accounting ❐ | 0 340 52876 1 | Successful Presentation ❐ |
| 0 340 63153 8 | Managing Information ❐ | 0 340 64761 2 | Successful Problem-Solving ❐ |
| 0 340 62737 9 | Succeeding at Interviews ❐ | 0 340 65563 1 | Successful Process Management ❐ |
| 0 340 60896 X | Successful Appraisals ❐ | 0 340 56531 4 | Successful Project Management ❐ |
| 0 340 60893 5 | Successful Assertiveness ❐ | 0 340 56479 2 | Successful Public Relations ❐ |
| 0 340 57640 5 | Successful Budgeting ❐ | 0 340 62738 7 | Successful Purchasing ❐ |
| 0 340 59813 1 | Successful Business Writing ❐ | 0 340 57523 9 | Successful Selling ❐ |
| 0 340 59855 7 | Successful Career Planning ❐ | 0 340 57889 0 | Successful Stress Management ❐ |
| 0 340 62032 3 | Successful Computing for Business ❐ | 0 340 64342 0 | Successful Teambuilding ❐ |
| 0 340 62740 9 | Successful Customer Care ❐ | 0 340 58763 6 | Successful Time Management ❐ |
| 0 340 63154 6 | Successful Decision-Making ❐ | 0 340 61889 2 | Successful Training ❐ |
| 0 340 62741 7 | Successful Direct Mail ❐ | 0 340 62103 6 | Understanding Benchmarking ❐ |
| 0 340 64330 7 | Successful Empowerment ❐ | 0 340 62103 6 | Understanding BPR ❐ |
| 0 340 64337 4 | Successful Environmental | 0 340 66444 4 | Understanding Business on |
| | Management ❐ | | the Internet ❐ |
| 0 340 65487 2 | Successful HRM ❐ | 0 340 56850 X | Understanding Just in Time ❐ |
| 0 340 59812 3 | Successful Interviewing ❐ | 0 340 61888 4 | Understanding Quality Management |
| 0 340 60895 1 | Successful Leadership ❐ | | Standards ❐ |
| 0 340 65503 8 | Successfully Managing Change ❐ | 0 340 65504 6 | Understanding Statistics ❐ |
| 0 340 57466 6 | Successful Market Research ❐ | 0 340 58764 4 | Understanding Total Quality |
| 0 340 55539 4 | Successful Marketing ❐ | | Management ❐ |
| 0 340 60894 3 | Successful Meetings ❐ | 0 340 62102 8 | Understanding VAT ❐ |
| 0 340 61137 5 | Successful Mentoring ❐ | | |

*All Hodder & Stoughton books are available from your local bookshop or can be ordered direct from the publisher. Just tick the titles you want and fill in the form below. Prices and availability subject to change without notice.*

To: Hodder & Stoughton Ltd, Cash Sales Department, Bookpoint, 39 Milton Park, Abingdon, Oxon, OX14 4TD. If you have a credit card you may order by telephone – 01235 831700.
Please enclose a cheque or postal order made payable to Bookpoint Ltd to the value of the cover price and allow the following for postage and packaging:
UK & BFPO: £1.00 for the first book, 50p for the second book and 30p for each additional book ordered up to a maximum charge of £3.00.
OVERSEAS & EIRE: £2.00 for the first book, £1.00 for the second book and 50p for each additional book.

Name:....................................................................................................................

Address: ................................................................................................................

................................................................................................................................

If you would prefer to pay by credit card, please complete:

Please debit my Visa/Mastercard/Diner's Card/American Express (delete as appropriate) card no:

☐☐☐☐☐☐☐☐☐☐☐☐☐☐☐☐

Signature .......................................................... Expiry Date ....................................